THE COMPLETE SAXOPHONE PLAYER

BOOK 3

by Raphael Ravenscroft.

Wise Publications
London/New York/Sydney

Exclusive Distributors:

Music Sales Limited
8/9 Frith Street, London W1V 5TZ, England.

Music Sales Corporation
257 Park Avenue South, New York, NY 10010, USA.

Music Sales Pty. Limited
120 Rothschild Avenue, Rosebery, NSW 2018, Australia.

This book © Copyright 1987 by
Wise Publications
ISBN 0.7119. 0889.3
Order No. AM 62738

Book designed by Sands Straker.
Cover designed by Pearce Marchbank.
Engraved by Music Print.
Typeset by Capital Setters.

Music Sales complete catalogue lists thousands of titles
and is free from your local music book shop, or direct
from Music Sales Limited.
Please send a cheque or postal order for £1.50 for postage to
Music Sales Limited, 8/9 Frith Street, London W1V 5TZ, England.

Printed in England by
Halstan & Co. Limited, Amersham, Bucks.

Contents

The Songs

About This Book

This is the Third Book in the exciting new series *The Complete Saxophone Player.* Great care has been taken to ensure that you find it as rewarding as the first two books in the series.

In *Book Three,* as in *Books One* and *Two,* you are helped by the easy-to-follow text combined with numerous clear diagrams. This series is of special value to people working on their own.

Carefully follow the sessions and by the end of the book you will find that you have made excellent progress in *Reading Music* and in *Technique.* You will be delighted too, to find that you have built up a fine and varied repertoire.

Remember to play regularly every day, if only for a short time. I have found that *little* and *often* is an excellent way of making rapid progress towards becoming *The Complete Saxophone Player.*

Lastly, *listening* to as much recorded saxophone music as possible is as important as playing itself. *Listening* gives you new ideas and expands your playing horizons.

Good luck in Book Three . . .

Raphael Ravenscroft

Session 1: Low Note Production

Before showing you how to play the two lowest notes, B natural and B flat, we must discuss the *low note* production technique.

Full sounding low notes are achieved by *lowering the jaw* slightly, without changing the embouchure, as you move down the scale. Don't worry! with just a little practice you will find this is the *only* way to produce a full sound in the lowest register and you will soon get a *feel* for where the jaw should be.

Okay, on to the new notes:

Low B natural is written and fingered like this:

Low B

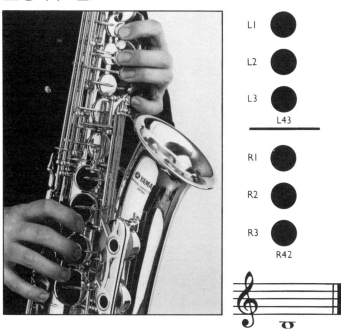

Low B flat (A♯) is written and fingered like this:

Low B♭

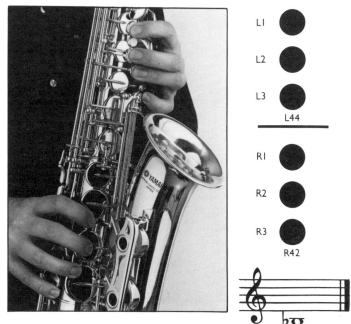

Now one of my favourite songs. It includes a few low
'honks'!

Lullaby of Birdland

Music by George Shearing. Words by David Weiss

Lul - la - by of Bird-land   that's what I ___   al - ways hear ___   when you sigh. ___

Nev - er in my word-land   could there   be ways to   re - veal ___   in   a   phrase how I   feel!

Have you ev - er heard two   tur - tle doves ___   bill   and   coo ___   when they love? ___

That's the kind of ma - gic   mus-ic   we make with our   lips ___   when we   kiss. ___

And there's a weep-y old   wil - low; ___   he real - ly knows how to   cry!

That's how I'd cry in my   pil - low ___   if   you should tell me fare - well and good-bye!

Lul - la - by of Bird-land,   whis - per low, ___   kiss   of sweet ___   and we'll go. ___

1.

Fly - in' high in Bird-land, high in the sky up a - bove ___ all be - cause we're in love.

2.

bove ___ all be - cause ___ we're in love. ___

6

Session 2: Sight Reading

As I mentioned earlier, *sight reading* should be included as part of your daily routine. I always try to get through to the end of a piece before going back and correcting any mistakes. This ensures that an element of flow is maintained in my playing. A useful hint is to read the notes slightly *ahead* of the ones you are playing.

Golden Rule
Try to read ahead

Sight-reading will become important as you begin to play with others more often. You will improve it steadily if you read through as much new material as possible. Don't rush, sight-reading is dependent on a lot more than just notes. It improves with every new scale, riff and song learned.

I suggest you memorise some of your favourite pieces, or even extracts of pieces. These fragments stand you in good stead when you 'take a solo'.

Try this piece of sight reading, it's that famous Beatles hit 'Eleanor Rigby'.

Eleanor Rigby
Words & Music by John Lennon & Paul McCartney

7

Session 3: New Note 'A♭' '(G♯)'

Learning the position and fingering of this note will enable you to play the scale of E flat major.

The note A Flat (G Sharp) is written and fingered like this:

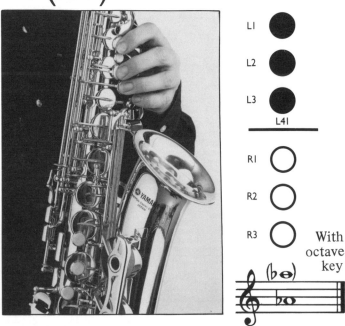

Let's play this song using the new fingering.

I Left My Heart In San Francisco
Words by Douglas Cross. Music by George Cory

I left my heart in San Fran - cis - co. ____

High on a hill it calls to me.

To be where lit - tle ca - ble cars _____ climb half way to the stars

the morn-ing fog may chill the air I don't care. My love waits

there in San Fran - cis - co _____ a - bove the

blue and wind - y sea. When I come

home to you San - Fran - cis - co _____ your gol - den

sun will shine for me. _____

Session 4: Scale Patterns

Learning the note A flat (G♯) enables you to play *all* the major scales. Look at the list below showing the scales we haven't encountered so far:

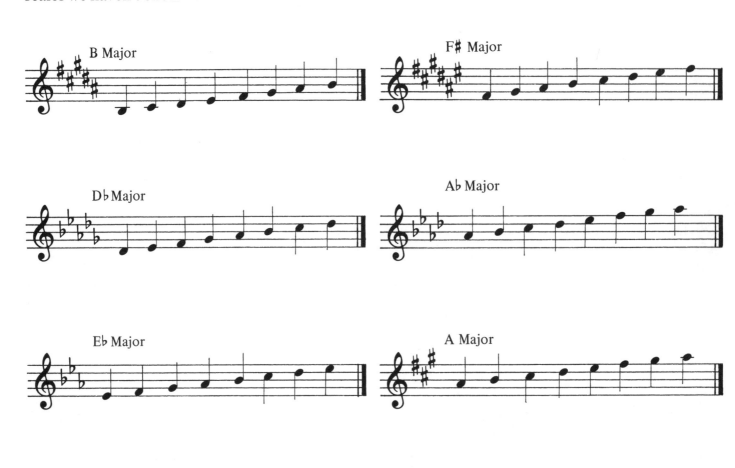

Phew! I thought I'd never get through that lot.

Session 5: Music Containing Different Time Signatures

This beautiful theme tune from the film of the same name is a good example of a piece of music using bars with different time signatures.
Remember that the 'pulse' of the music stays the same. Only the number of beats in the bars alters.

A Man and a Woman

Music by Francis Lai
Original Words by Pierre Barough
English Lyric by Jerry Keller

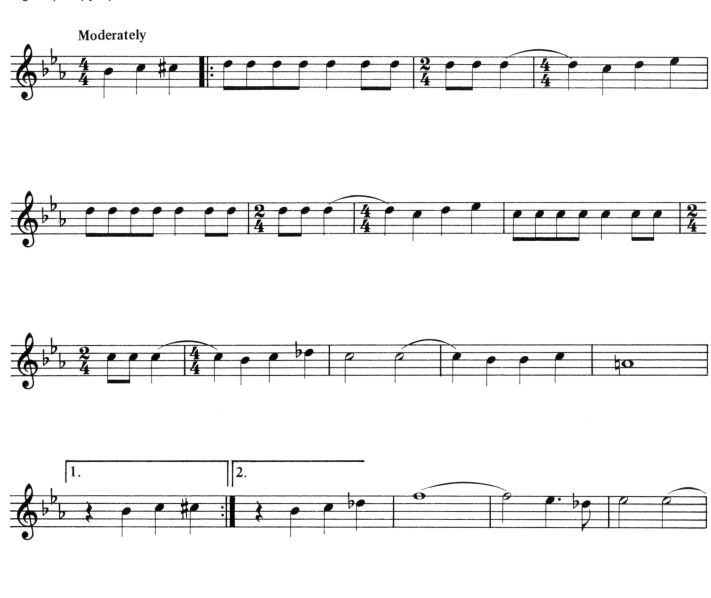

Session 6: Key Signatures, Dotted Quavers And Semi Quavers

Before I list the key signatures of all the *major* keys, I will give you a rule of thumb that enables you to work out the order of sharps and flats as they occur. This device is called the *'circle of fifths'* and although it has fairly wide ramifications in regard to the creation and resolution of tension, it should be understood by all players at an early stage. I shall go into details regarding its wider implications in *Book Four.* For now, let's have a look at the diagram.

The reason why the keys are ordered in this way is connected with the fact that each successive step (following the direction of the arrows), represents the most obvious path of resolution, i.e. C (or C seventh) will resolve to F. F (or F seventh) will resolve to B Flat and so the circle continues.

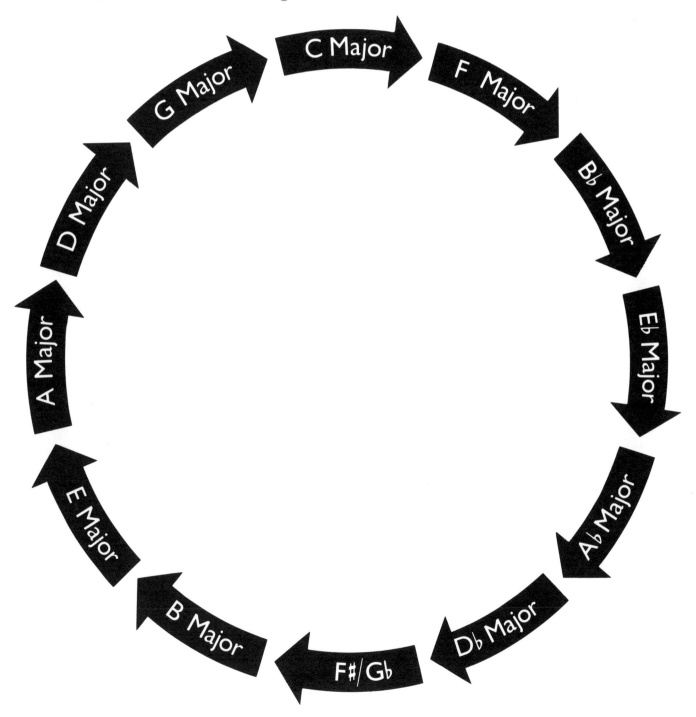

Key Signatures

Here is a list of all the major *key signatures* structured according to the Circle of Fifths diagram. Notice how each successive step along the Circle of Fifths is five notes higher than the last.

The scales of F♯ and G♭ major are comprised of the same notes, but they have different names.

Session 7: Dotted Quavers And Semi Quavers

In Book One, you learned to divide crotchets into quavers.

We can now divide the quavers into semiquavers (or sixteenth notes)

This means we have four quavers to a crotchet.

And this is three semiquavers tied together.

Practise this rhythm by first tapping four taps to a crotchet beat.

1 2 3 4 1 2 3 4 1 2 3 4 1 2 3 4

Now tap only the first and fourth while thinking through the other two.

It will of course be written like this . . .

or

We can count it like this . . .

1 & 2 3 & 4 3 & 4 4 & 4

Dotted quaver and semiquaver rests are, of course, counted in exactly the same way as dotted quavers and semiquavers.

Note that the phrasing

is simply

played with reversed timing. ie

Session 8: Staccato

Knowledge of the functions of the tongue in playing i.e. regulating the strokes with precision, is the key to good *staccato* playing.

The correct tonguing procedure for staccato playing requires independent control of the front portion of the tongue. Try tonguing 'Ta-Ta-Ta' using short strokes, without changing the rest of the embouchure.

The sign for *staccato* is a dot placed over a note. This has the effect of approximately *halving* the length of the written note. So, a dot placed over a *crotchet* (quarter note) would become a *quaver* (eighth note). Likewise, a dot placed over a *quaver* (eighth note) would become a *semiquaver* (sixteenth note).

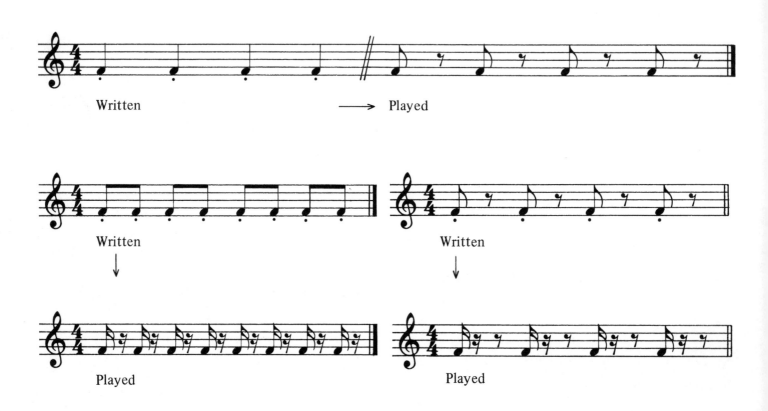

Try this well known jazz favourite, playing the
notes with *dots* over them with only *half* their
written value. (Staccato)

Take The 'A' Train
Words & Music by Billy Strayhorn

Here it is at last! The tune I know you have been
waiting for. It should ideally be played on *Tenor
Sax.*

The Pink Panther Theme

Words & Music by Henry Mancini

Session 9: Palm Keys (New Notes From 'High D' To 'High F')

You have no doubt experimented with these keys already. The high register notes require very relaxed fingers in order to allow the instrument to sing out. The high D key is depressed with the inside of the left index finger

High D Key = LPK1 (■)

The note D is written and fingered like this:

D

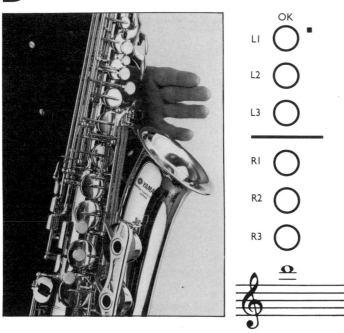

It is accepted practice to drop the *left* hand slightly, lowering it gently on to the key (allowing the wrist to 'break'). Do not press inward with the palm when playing the note D.

The note *E flat* (D♯) is played pressing the high E flat and D keys with the left index finger.

High Eb Key = LPK2 (◆)

E♭

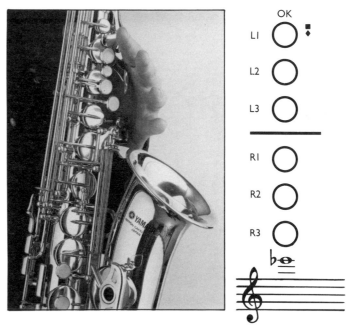

The note E natural is played by pressing the high D, and E flat, with the side of the right hand index finger (R1) pressing the high E key.

High E Key = RSK1

E Natural

Ensure you have a fluid *right* hand, moving it smoothly from its position over the low register F, E and D keys up to the high E key and back. Try not to jerk this movement, as this is one of the chief causes of uneven playing in the high register.

The note F   is written and fingered like this:

★ = LPK3

F

It is most important to feel comfortable when playing higher notes. Consequently, *economy* of movement is vital.

Remember not to tense-up when playing in the higher register. The tone will only sound rich and full if your embouchure and fingers are as relaxed as possible, giving the instrument its full potential to vibrate.

This song utilises the high register of the
instrument.

A Whiter Shade Of Pale

Words & Music by Keith Reid & Gary Brooker

We skipped the light fan - dan-go ___ and turned cart-wheels 'cross the floor ___

I was feel-ing kind of sea - sick ___ but the crowd called out for more. ___

___ The room was hum-ming hard - er ___ as the ceil -ing flew a - way ___ cresc. . . . .

When we called out for an - oth - er drink. ___ the wait- er brought a tray. ___ And so it

was ___ that la - ter as the mil - ler told his tale ___

that her face at first just ghost-ly ___ turned a whi - ter ___ shade of pale. ___

Session 10: Vibrato

Although there are different schools of thought on this aspect of playing, it is generally held that most saxophone players use vibrato in some form or other. Many players, including myself, feel that vibrato is the life-blood of the tone.

The important benefits of using vibrato include:

1) Improved *tone* quality
2) Better *pitch* control.

In essence, *vibrato* is controlled pitch fluctuation.

Three steps to *vibrato*.

1) Play a middle range note (A,B or C) then drop the jaw slightly. (wah)
2) Raise the jaw back to its original level. (oou)

Note: When you dropped your jaw, you lowered the pitch slightly and when you raised your jaw you returned the pitch to its original level. These are the simple mechanics behind vibrato technique.

3) Carry out steps one and two '*in time*'.

Follow the next diagram.

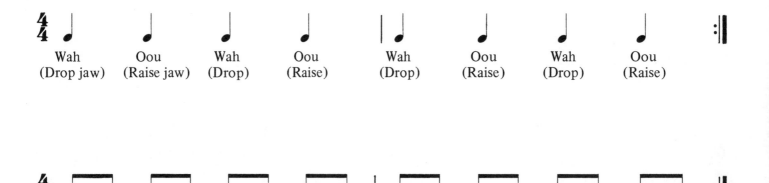

This piece would be lifeless were it not for the use of *vibrato*. Look at the small notes before the note F in bar two. These are called *grace notes* and are squeezed in just before the beat.

The Old Castle (from Pictures At An Exhibition)

By Modest Petrovitch Mussorgsky

Slow—with feeling

Session 11: Further Tonguing Procedures

As we have already discussed, the use of the tongue to start a note is called the attack. Conversely, the termination of a note is called the release.

The Release

This has special problems which are sometimes neglected. These include alteration of pitch, spreading tone and poor timing. The most important aspect of the release is to place the tongue tip cleanly back on to the reed, always ensuring that the air-stream from your lungs is maintained.

I have found that the *release,* like the attack, is best rehearsed with a rhythmic pulse in mind.

Try this tune – it's an Ellington swing hit.

Perdido

Music by Juan Tizol. Words by Harry Lenk & Ervin Drake

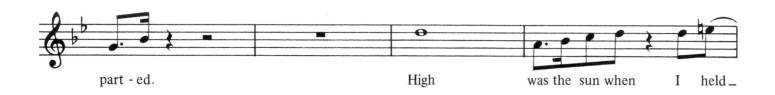

part - ed. High was the sun when I held

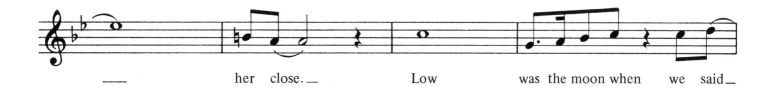

her close. Low was the moon when we said

"A - dios." Per - di - do my heart ev - er since is Per -

di - do, I know I must go to Tor - ri - do, to

find what I lost Per - di - do!

Session 12: Three Irish Jigs

Remember: it's the *removal* of the tongue from the reed which starts the tone, assuming that the correct amount of air pressure is being applied at the point of the reed. After the attack, the tongue should remain at the bottom of the mouth cavity, close to the reed. This position will allow it to strike up and stop the sound.

Follow the interesting articulations in these three tunes:

1. The Tenpenny Bit

Traditional

2. The Irish Washerwoman

Traditional

Vivace ♪. = Fast

3. St Patrick's Day

Traditional

Session 13: Minor Scales

A minor scale is said to be *related* to a major scale as they both have the same key signature. Let us take the scale of G major as our example. All we have to do to find the relative minor scale is start a scale three semitones lower than G which in this case is E. Play up the G scale until we get to the *seventh* note, which is D, then *raise* (sharpen) this note and we have played the scale of *E minor*.

I have indicated the different intervals that make up the scales, as a series of *tones* (T) and *semitones* (S). Note that 3S equals three semitones.

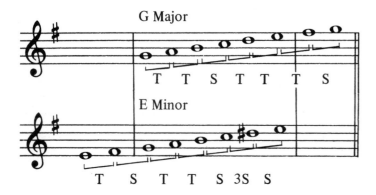

This form of the minor scale is called the *harmonic minor scale* and uses the same notes in its descending form.

Here is another example

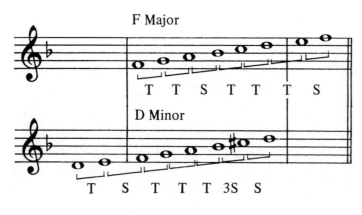

The most important difference between major and minor scales is the interval between the first and third notes. The major scales have an interval of two tones (four semitones) between the first and third notes. This is called a *major third*. Minor scales have an interval of a tone and a half (three semitones) between the first and third notes. This is called a *minor third*. It is the minor third which gives minor scales (and chords) their 'sad' sound.

Here are all the harmonic scales which have key signatures in which you have played so far. Practise them, taking note of the similarity to their relative major key.

All the harmonic minor scales can be found at the back of this book.

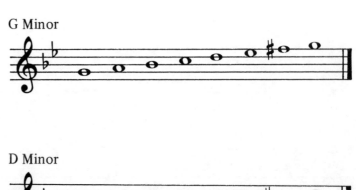

A Minor

Melodic Minor Scales

To construct a *melodic* minor scale in its ascending form we take a harmonic minor scale;

A minor (harmonic).

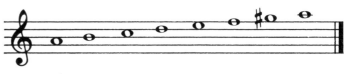

E Minor

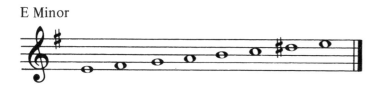

The sixth note is raised by a semitone and the scale becomes:

A minor (melodic)(ascending).

B Minor

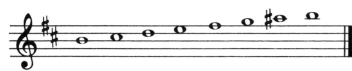

The descending form of the melodic minor scale uses the same notes as its relative major, but uses a different section of the scale.
Look at the following example.

F♯ Minor

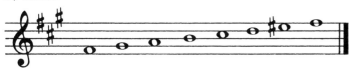

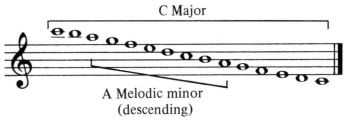

C♯ Minor

To sum up, here is the scale of A melodic minor in its ascending and descending forms showing the tonal intervals.

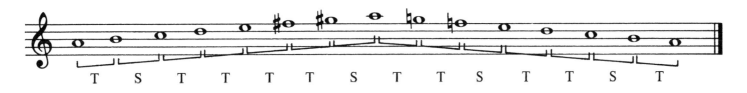

Using the preceding information you can now construct all the melodic minor scales.

Now play this well known theme from the popular
TV series. Remember, look at the key and the layout
before you start playing. (I'll give you a hint – it's in a
minor key).

Hawaii Five-0

By Mort Stevens

Session 14: Patterns – Introduction To Improvisation

As an introduction to *improvising* it is important to realise that you can 'break' any *scale* down into *chords*. These are the essential notes that determine the 'character' of a scale.

A chord consists of a *'pile of notes'*. The most simple *'pile'* is built up using the 1st, 3rd and 5th note of *any* scale. This we call a *triad*. Hence in the key of *C major*, the *C major triad* looks like this:

C minor would look like this:

Let's use this knowledge to create a very simple pattern.

The letters above each bar are called *chord symbols*. They are a 'shorthand' method of denoting basic chordal harmony and will be explained more fully later on.

Start by looking at the chord progression as a whole. Look at the key (generally the first chord of the piece).

This will indicate the notes needed to create tension and relaxation. Begin by playing chord notes only, like this:

What happens if you play a non-chord note? Try this
example and find out:

As you have seen, the tension created by any *non-chord note,* can be resolved by moving on to its
adjacent *chord note.* Try a chorus for yourself.

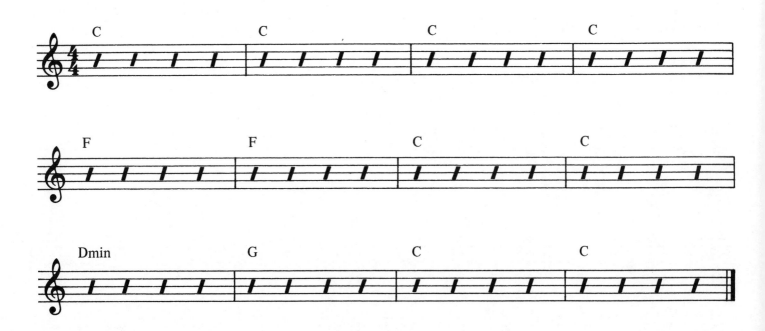

Session 15: Seventh Chords

As you can well imagine, music does not consist only of creating and resolving tension to *basic* triadic notes. There are many chord variations using the basic triadic notes as a starting point. For example, if we pile another third on to the existing pile of thirds (notes 1, 3 & 5), we get a *major seventh chord*.

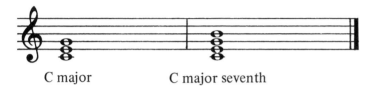

     C major   C major seventh

To add further variety, we could raise or lower any of the notes in the chord by half a tone. Only the root (or first note) must remain the same. (C in *C major* etc.) as this note determines the basic key. Varying the notes of the chord produces some interesting effects, and introduces new possibilities to the soloist or composer.

Look at the following examples, taking note of how the original chord notes have been changed.

Firstly the *triad:*

Now the *seventh* chord.

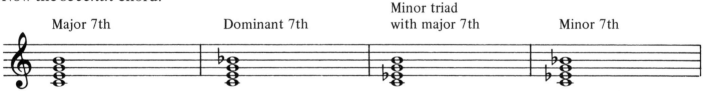

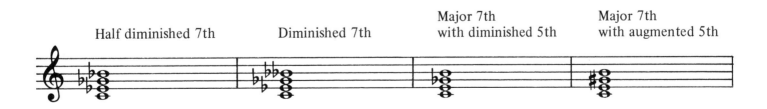

Symbols

Chord symbols, as explained earlier, can be used as a shorthand method of conveying the intention of the composer. Here are the most common *chord symbols* and examples of how they would affect chords in the key of *D major*.

D Major: Dma, DM

D Diminished: Ddim, D°

D 7th; D7

D Minor: Dmi, D−,

D Diminished 7th: Ddim 7,D°7

D Minor 7th: Dmi7,Dm7,D−7.

D Augmented: Daug, D+

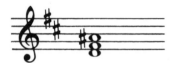

D Major 7th: DMa7, DM7,D°7

D Half-diminished 7th: Dm7-5, DM Ø

The *seventh* notes in this famous 'bluesy' piece are circled. See what effect they have and how they are resolved. I have indicated the resolutions of the seventh notes by the use of arrows on the music.

Georgia On My Mind

Words by Stuart Garrell. Music by Hoagy Carmichael

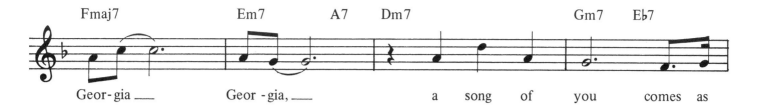

Geor-gia ___ Geor-gia, ___ a song of you comes as

sweet and clear ___ as moon-light on the ___ pines. _____

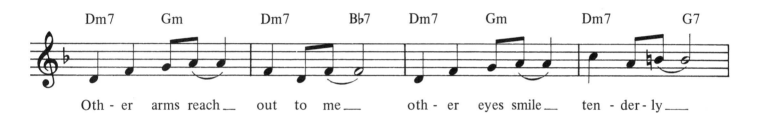

Oth-er arms reach ___ out to me ___ oth-er eyes smile ___ ten-der-ly ___

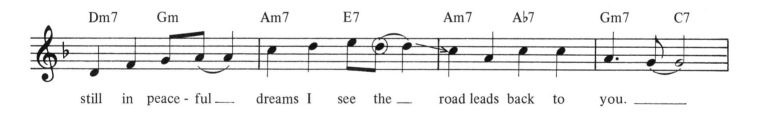

still in peace-ful ___ dreams I see the ___ road leads back to you. _____

Geor-gia ___ Geor-gia, ___ no peace I find, ___ just an

old sweet song ___ keeps Geor-gia on my ___ mind.

Session 16: Blues

Most people perform their first solo improvisations over the *blues* sequence. It represents one of the earliest and most widely used jazz forms.

The *blues* sequence has a 12-bar form, meaning that it repeats a set of chord changes 12 bars in length. So, the blues in D would look like this:

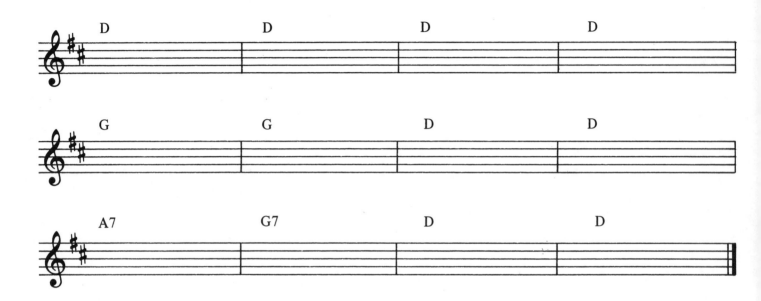

Why not familiarise yourself with the chordal notes of this sequence, playing simple patterns like this:

Now try the same idea using non-chord notes to
create contrast and varied pace. Something like
this:

Try it on your own now. I don't expect a Parker
or Coltrane, just keep it simple and think of
developing a motive or idea.

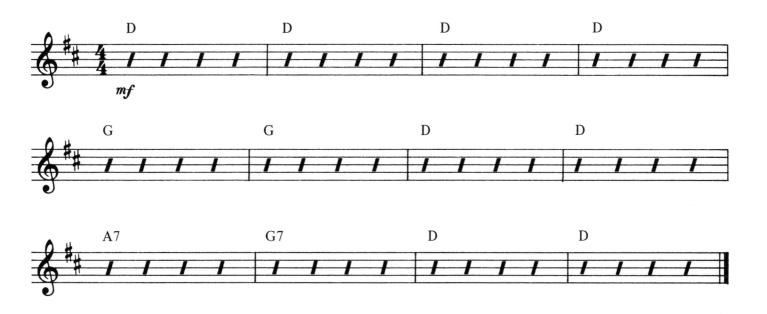

Session 17: Swing

Swing, in jazz, has to do with our personal feelings towards music. By this I mean: jazz lovers and people who listen to jazz will approach playing with very different ideas from people who only listen to rock. Their ideas on phrasing and dynamics will understandably be very different. Consequently, swing is very difficult to put into words, save to say it is best thought of as *rhythmic tension* created at the discretion of the performer.

The way we create and resolve this rhythmic tension, is rooted in our appreciation and experience of 'live' or recorded music. Consequently, each jazz soloist has his or her own way of 'swinging' and for many players this element becomes their own jazz 'thumbprint'.

Swing, then, allows us the freedom to interpret any piece of music from the heaviest classical to the lightest pop tune, with a *jazz* feel. This can be very simply demonstrated in the two following examples. They are the same piece of music written out in two different styles.

Before attempting this variation, note that:

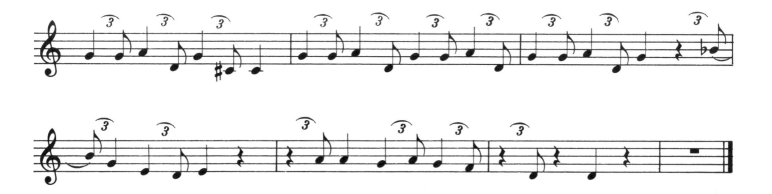

On the surface, the subdivision of the beat seems just to have converted the 4/4 feel into a 12/8 feel i.e. the rhythmic subdivision of each beat is broken up into triplets.

But, although the beat may *appear* to be divided into three equal sub-divisions, to make it sound really *jazzy* you would have to close your eyes and sing (or play) it the way *you* want to hear it. This entails breaking away from all the rhythmic conventions described so far.

Consequently, one interpretation might look like this. . .

As you can see from the above example it is not viable to notate jazz like this. Not only is it difficult to read, but it also places jazz into a strait jacket. So, what we are called on to do as jazz players is to *interpret* what we read, rather than just reproduce the same result time after time.

Session 18: Jazz Soloing

I suggest you get hold of a copy of Billy Joel's album *'The Stranger'*, and listen to the saxophone playing. 'Just The Way You Are', from this album, is written out below. Follow the music carefully, ensuring that you understand how each of the musical phrases is played.

Phil Woods, the saxophone player, delivers what must be just about the 'perfect' solo for the idiom. Remember, it has taken him *years* to get to the point at which he can produce such an effective solo of this *simplicity*. Listen to his *sound* and interpretation a few times, then try it for yourself. (I have written out only the saxophone solo).

Just The Way You Are
Words & Music by Billy Joel

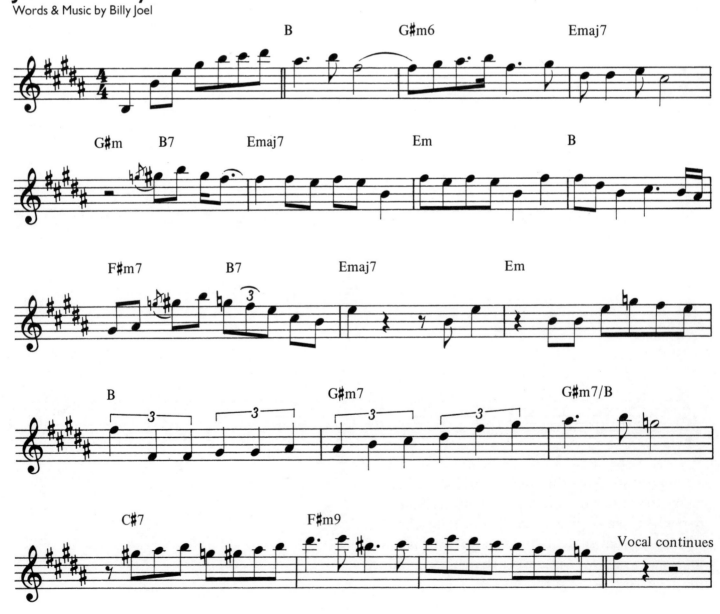

Vocal continues

Try to memorise this blues tune, then play it
through using your own interpretation of the chord
symbols.

The Creole Love Call

Words & Music by Duke Ellington

As you become more experienced you will begin to
pick up the subtleties of phrasing of both pitch and
rhythm that go to make up the character of a piece.

Session 19: More Jazz Solos

Another style of playing is the smooth *'jazz influenced'* style used so prominently by soloists on *'fusion'* albums. This next solo is by Grover Washington, Jr and is taken from his album 'Winelight'.

The solo occurs twice in the song, once in the middle register and once in the upper register.

I suggest you try the middle register version first. The phrasing of the solo is quite complicated. If you have trouble reading it, try writing it out, doubling the duration of each note. This is a very good way of simplifying difficult passages:

Note that using this technique turns one bar into two. e.g. (first bar of solo becomes)

Just The Two Of Us

Words & Music by Ralph MacDonald,
William Salter & Bill Withers

The ╱ sign you encounter in this piece means that you start the note it precedes a little flat, and then 'slide' up to the correct pitch.

Sax solo. (middle register)

Sax solo. (upper register)

The time has come folks!!! Time to blow my own trumpet (or in this case – saxophone). Once again listen to the original record *(Baker Street)* and the version by the London Symphony Orchestra (Classic Rock). This is a prime example of the differences in the technique demanded of the modern day session player. Notice how the two versions contrast with one another. I found playing with the L.S.O. more difficult than doing the original with Gerry, but I must say gigging with a 160 piece *'band'* does have its merits.

Try it for yourself . . .

Baker Street
Words & Music by Gerry Rafferty

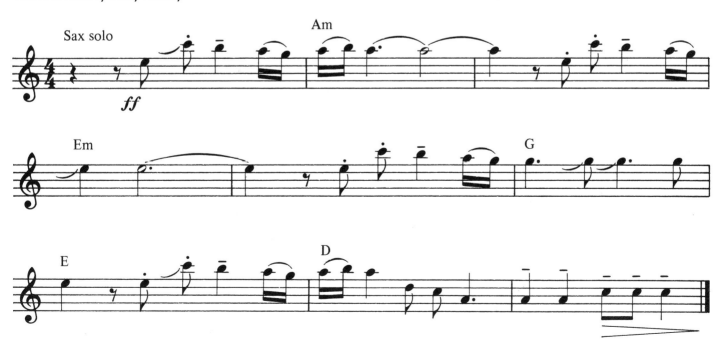

Summary Of Book Three

You have now reached a new high point in your playing and I intend to sustain this momentum in Book 4.

You can play *all* the most used notes on the instrument, both high and low.

I have given you a technique to use as an aid to better *sight reading*.

We have examined the derivation of all the *Scales* and their related *Key Signatures*.

I have put forward ideas on the use of *Vibrato* and *Vibrato Technique*.

We have examined the derivation of all the *Scales* and their related *Key Signatures*.

You now know all the *Major* and *Minor Scales* and *Chords* to use in conjunction with *Patterns* in the initial stages of *Improvisation*.

We have examined the derivation of the *Blues* as a stepping stone to the more involved improvising forms. These are discussed in the next book.

I have explained the concept of *Swing* and have pointed out the importance of its correct usage in *Jazz*.

You have extended your *Popular Song* and *Jazz* repertoire with many new songs.

Comprehensive Scale Chart

The sign you will encounter in the scale of G sharp minor means that the note so designated is raised by two semitones. This sign is called the *Double Sharp*.

C♭ Major

C Major

B Major

F Major

E Major

B♭ Major

A Major

E♭ Major

D Major

A♭ Major

G Major

MINOR SCALES

D♭ Major

A Minor (harmonic)

G♭ Major

D Minor (harmonic)

G Minor (harmonic)

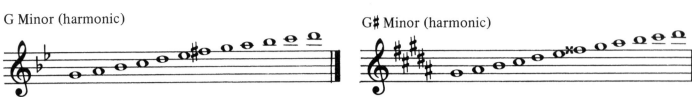

G♯ Minor (harmonic)

C Minor (harmonic)

C♯ Minor (harmonic)

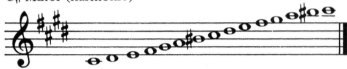

F Minor (harmonic)

F♯ Minor (harmonic)

B♭ Minor (harmonic)

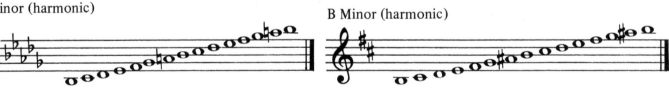

B Minor (harmonic)

E♭ Minor (harmonic)

E Minor (harmonic)

A♭ Minor (harmonic)

Observations On Book Three

In *Book Three* I have laid the groundwork for some of the techniques to be explored in *Book Four*.

The popular music scene, being what it is, is ever changing. It is for this reason that I have incorporated the most up-to-date elements and theories.

If you haven't done so already, I suggest you start trying out different mouthpieces, mouthpiece-reed combinations and even *Saxophones!*

Don't neglect the *electronic* developments made available in the last year or so. Many saxophonists are now using affordable electronic effects to enhance their playing.

After *Book Four* I intend to compile a series of song-books including the most important pieces from Jazz, Pop and Classical Repertoire. These will enable you to expand your playing horizons in any of these particular directions.

Move on to *Book Four* now and let's get professional.